Are you an Ant?

For the children and staff of the
Wandle Primary School, Wandsworth – J.A. and T.H.

KINGFISHER
Kingfisher Publications Plc
New Penderel House
283–288 High Holborn
London WC1V 7HZ
www.kingfisherpub.com

First published by Kingfisher Publications Plc 2002

3 5 7 9 10 8 6 4 2

1SWK/0402/TWP/GRS/150ENSOMA

A CIP catalogue record for this book is available from
the British Library.

ISBN 0 7534 0551 2

Editor: Carron Brown
Series Designer: Jane Buckley

Printed in Singapore

Up the Garden Path

Are You an Ant?

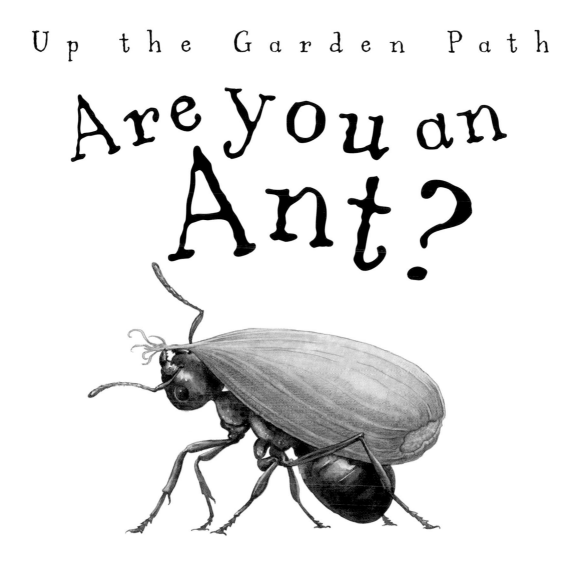

Judy Allen and Tudor Humphries

KINGfISHER

Are you an ant?

If you are,
your mother is a queen.

One hot summer day she went
on a mating flight with
thousands of others so that
she would be able to lay eggs.

Afterwards she flew down
to the ground. She knew she
didn't need her wings any more,
so she took them off.

Then she dug herself a small room
under the earth.

Now she is in her room,
the queen begins to lay eggs.
You are in one of them.
Hatch out of the egg
as soon as you can.

You don't look like an ant yet.

You're a grub, and you're hungry.

There are eggs all over the place.

Eat some. It's all right, they won't mind.

They're only eggs.

Soon, you must change into a pupa.
A pupa is a bit like an egg, only bigger.
When you're ready, break out!

You look almost like an ant – but
you're white and soft.

Don't worry.
Slowly your skin will become hard
and black and you'll look perfect.
There are lots of others like you.
You are one of a big family.
You are a worker!

Work hard to build a nest.
Dig storerooms and nurseries
and bedrooms and corridors.

It's all right, you don't have to work alone. The others will work with you.

You haven't got any voices, but you can talk to each other by touching feelers.

11

Don't eat any more eggs.
Go out and hunt for food.
Seeds are nice. So are bugs
and woodlice. Springtails
are delicious, but hard to
catch because they jump.

Bite your prey and spray
it with acid from your tail.
Actually, you're not a very
good hunter. Look out
for bugs that have been
trodden on. They're easy.

You may think there's easy food in kitchens, but be careful. There are crumbs and grains of sugar, which is nice. There are also people, and that's not so nice.

People don't like you in their homes.
They may squash you. They may poison
you. Or they may sweep the floor so you
can't find anything to eat.

The best food is honeydew.
It comes from aphids.
Find a plant with aphids
feeding on it.

March up the stem
with the other workers.
Now stroke an aphid until
it gives you a drop of honeydew.

It's a bit like milking
a cow, but you wouldn't
know about that, you're an ant.

Look after your aphids.

Ladybirds eat aphids – so
watch out for ladybird
eggs and throw them away.

You must take food
back to the nest.

Some you can lift.

Some you can drag.

Some you can put in your second stomach. It's called a crop and it's very useful for carrying spare food home.

Back at the nest,
there's plenty to do.
Feed the queen –
who is still laying eggs.
Feed the grubs –
who are still hatching.

Look after
the eggs and grubs.
When it's cold, carry them
deep into the nest where it's cosy.
When the sun warms the earth,
carry them up near the surface.

Oh – and don't forget to take
out the garbage.

21

Life isn't all food and work.
There's danger, too.
Birds and lizards and toads
think you are good
to eat.

Some birds
pick you up and push
you under their wings.
Why? Because the acid in your
body kills the ticks that bite
them and make them itch.
This is called anting.

Anting is nice for birds.
Anting is not nice for ants.

23

However, if your family looks a bit

like this

or this

24

or this

you are not an ant.

You are...

25

...a human child.

You don't have
to look after eggs
and grubs.

You don't have
to milk aphids.

And you probably don't
have to march in a line
with lots of others.

Never mind, you can do
a great many things that
ants can't do.

Best of all, no bird is ever,
ever, EVER going to pick
you up in its beak and
stuff you under its wing.

Did You Know...

...the ants in this book are black garden ants, but there are about 10,000 different kinds of ant, living all over the world.

...some grow their own food – South American leafcutter ants carry bits of leaf home and chew them up to make compost for their fungus gardens.

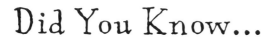

...some are hunters – African driver ants march in their thousands in long columns. They will eat any animal in their path if it doesn't escape in time!

...some collect seeds and fruits and honeydew – these ants leave a scent trail to guide their sisters to the food.

...some ants can sting, so take care!